HOW IT HAPPENS
at the Truck Plant

By Jenna Anderson
Photographs by Bob and Diane Wolfe

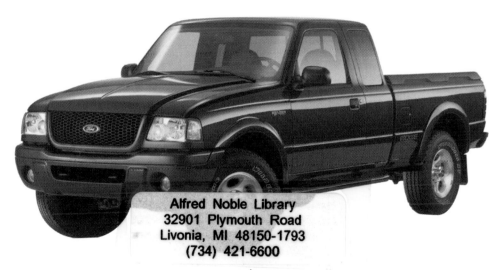

CLARA
HOUSE
BOOKS

Minneapolis

The publisher would like to thank the Ford Motor Company and its
employees for their generous help with this book.

Clara House Books
The Oliver Press, Inc.
Charlotte Square
5707 West 36th Street
Minneapolis, MN 55416-2510

Library of Congress Cataloging-in-Publication Data
Anderson, Jenna, 1977-
   How it happens at the truck plant / by Jenna Anderson ; photographs by Bob and Diane Wolfe.
       p. cm. — (How it happens)
   Summary: Photographs and text describe how pickup trucks are made.
   ISBN 1-881508-93-5 (lib. bdg.)
   1. Pickup trucks—Design and construction—Juvenile literature. 2. Assembly-line
methods—Juvenile literature. I. Wolfe, Diane. II. Wolfe, Robert L. III. Title. IV. Series.

TL278.A534 2002
629.223'2—dc21

                                                    2001053928

ISBN 1-881508-93-5
Printed in the United States of America
08 07 06 05 04 03 02   8 7 6 5 4 3 2 1

Millions of people rely on pickup trucks for transportation every day. These powerful vehicles are specially built to haul heavy trailers and carry large loads. But how do hundreds of small parts come together to make a big, tough truck? Taking you inside an assembly plant that builds nearly 1,000 trucks each day, this book will give you an up-close look at how a pickup truck takes shape, piece by piece.

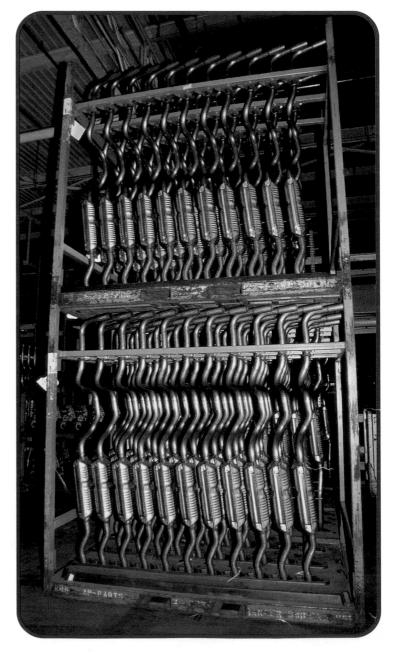

Parts

At the assembly plant, workers put many different parts together to make trucks. All of the parts—like the doors, mufflers, and tires shown at left—are made in other factories and shipped to the assembly plant by train. As shown below, workers use **forklifts** (machines that lift and carry heavy objects from place to place) to unload the parts from the train cars.

Body

The main structure of the truck is called the **body**. Most of the parts that make up the body are made of a hard, strong metal called **steel**. These parts are attached together by **welding**, or heating and melting them at the spot where they meet. When the metal cools and hardens again, the pieces will be firmly joined. A frame called a **buck** holds some of the pieces together while a worker welds them in place.

Most of the welding is done by **robots**, machines that can be programmed to perform complicated tasks. This robot is working on the **cab** of a truck (the front half of the body, where the driver and passengers sit).

There are more than 2,000 spot welds (places where the metal is welded together) in each truck.

When the welding is finished, the cab is joined with the **box** (the back half of the body) on a **skid**, or platform, that holds them in place as they move through the assembly process.

The workers shown at left are installing the truck's hood, which covers the space in the front of the truck where the engine will be. Below, another worker adds doors to the truck.

When the body is finished, workers hammer out any dents and sand away any scratches from the metal. They need to make sure that the surface of the truck is smooth before it is painted.

Paint

Each truck is treated with chemicals that clean it and prepare the metal for painting. Then, robots spray on a base coat of paint. The picture below shows a robot preparing to paint a truck. The robot in the background is programmed to open the doors of the truck so that other robots can paint the inside.

In the picture at left, a worker sprays the truck with a coat of colored paint. Finally, the robots shown below spray on a clear, glossy coating that will help to protect the paint from being scratched or chipped. The painted trucks will then be placed in a large, hot oven that dries the paint.

Trim

Now, workers begin to add details and accessories—called **trim**—to the truck. One of these is the **dashboard**, which fits in the inside front of the cab and holds storage compartments and instrument panels. The picture below shows what the unfinished dashboard looks like when it arrives at the assembly plant. At right, workers install the stereo (top) and steering wheel (bottom) in the dashboard.

When the dashboard is finished, it is installed in the cab of the truck.

The assembly plant makes more than one **model**, or kind, of truck, and each truck can have different features and accessories. A piece of paper taped to the truck tells the workers what the truck will be like—for example, whether to install a CD player and what color carpet to put inside.

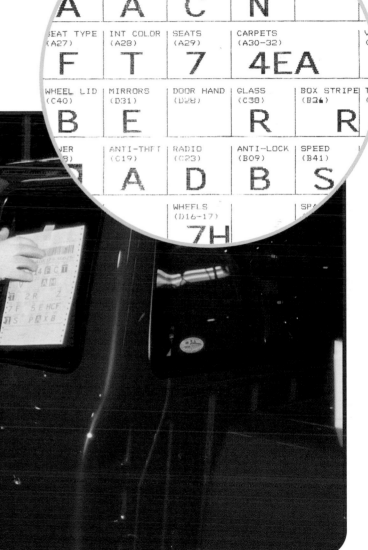

ENGINE SIZE (E03)			
E			

AUX COOL (F02)	FLEX FUEL (E12)	RADIATOR (F08)	
A	A	C	N

SEAT TYPE (A27)	INT COLOR (A28)	SEATS (A29)	CARPETS (A30-32)	V (L
F	T	7	4EA	

WHEEL LID (C40)	MIRRORS (D31)	DOOR HAND (D28)	GLASS (C38)	BOX STRIPE (B26)	TA (P
B	E		R	R	

ER 8)	ANTI-THEF (C19)	RADIO (C23)	ANTI-LOCK (B09)	SPEED (B41)
	A	D	B	S

WHEELS (D16-17)	SPA
7H	

A robot sets the windshield in place on the front of the truck.

Chassis

Meanwhile, in another part of the assembly plant, workers are preparing the **chassis** (CHASS-ee). This rectangular metal frame will support the body of the truck. It will also hold important parts like the **engine**, which powers the truck.

The picture below shows the engine being attached to the **transmission** (the cone-shaped part on the left), which will send the engine's power to the axles that turn the wheels. The finished engine is installed in the front of the chassis, as shown at right.

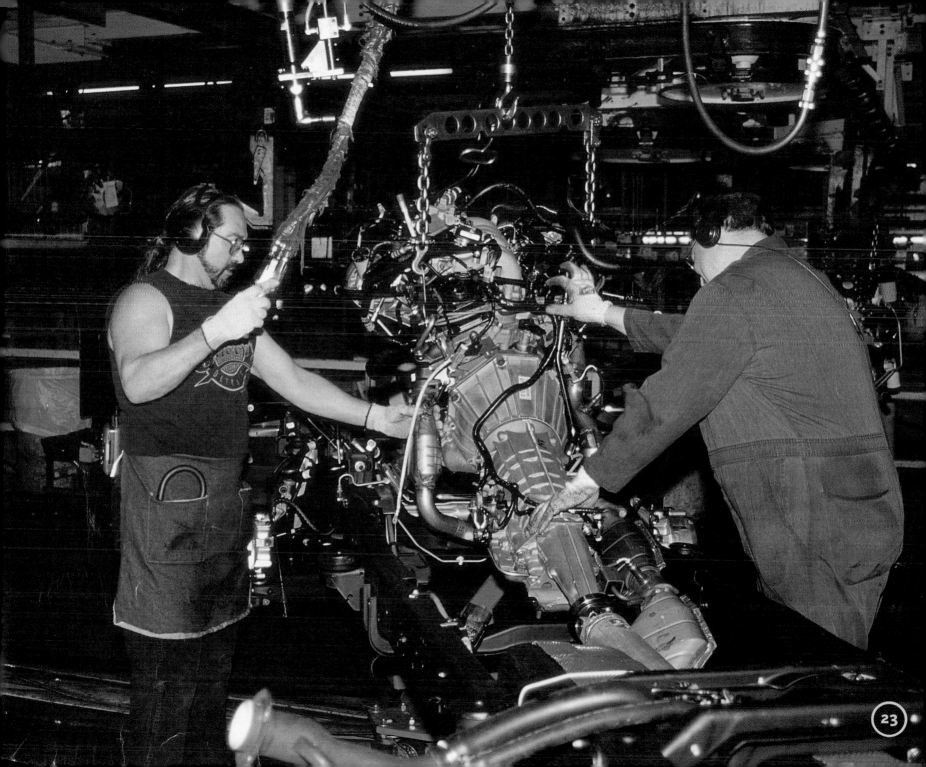

Other parts installed in the chassis include the brake system, the bumpers, and the axles (long metal rods that hold and turn the wheels).

A machine lifts the body of the truck off its skid and lowers it onto the finished chassis.

Finishing

Now the truck is nearly complete. Workers need to finish all the wiring and fill the truck up with gasoline, oil, brake fluid, and everything else needed to make it ready to drive. They also install the seats, as shown below. The pictures at right show the wheels being added to the truck.

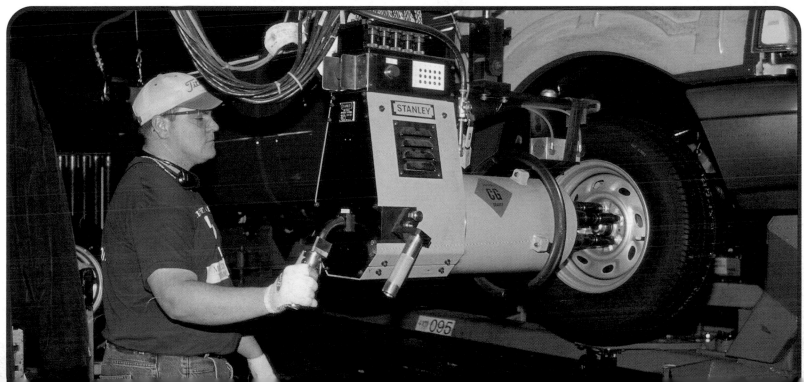

Testing

Each truck is carefully tested for quality. This truck is being soaked with water to check whether the doors and windows leak. In another test, trucks are held in place and then driven, without moving, at 60 miles per hour to check for any problems.

Workers check the trucks for leaks, squeaks, loose parts, and any other defects. They make sure that each truck has all the necessary parts and that every part works correctly.

Shipping

The trucks are driven out of the assembly plant into a huge parking lot. There, they will be loaded onto trucks or train cars that will transport them to truck dealerships (stores) throughout the country and the world.

Glossary

body: the main structure of a truck

box: the back part of the body of a truck, used for carrying cargo

buck: a frame that holds pieces of the body together while they are being welded

cab: the front part of the body of a truck, where the driver and passengers sit

chassis: a rectangular metal frame that supports the body of a truck and holds the parts and wiring necessary to make it run, including the engine and the wheels

dashboard: a piece that fits across the inside front of the cab of a truck, holding storage compartments, instrument panels, and the steering wheel

engine: the part that powers a truck

forklift: a machine that lifts and carries heavy objects from place to place

model: a style or design of an item

robot: a machine that can be programmed to perform complicated physical tasks

skid: the metal platform that holds the body of a truck in place as it moves through the assembly process

steel: a hard, strong metal

transmission: the part of a truck that sends the engine's power to the axles that turn the wheels

trim: details and accessories added to a truck

welding: a way of joining pieces of metal by heating them at the spot where they meet